THE CONSTITUTION EXPLAINED!

ARTICLE I

BUILDING THE CONGRESS

BY JULIA McDONNELL

Gareth Stevens PUBLISHING

Please visit our website, www.garethstevens.com. For a free color catalog of all our high-quality books, call toll free 1-800-542-2595 or fax 1-877-542-2596.

Cataloging-in-Publication Data

Names: McDonnell, Julia.
Title: Article I: building the Congress / Julia McDonnell.
Description: New York : Gareth Stevens Publishing, 2021. | Series: The Constitution explained! | Includes glossary and index.
Identifiers: ISBN 9781538258507 (pbk.) | ISBN 9781538258521 (library bound) | ISBN 9781538258514 (6 pack)
Subjects: LCSH: United States. Constitution–Juvenile literature. | Constitutional history–United States–Juvenile literature.
Classification: LCC E303.M394 2021 | DDC 342.7302'9–dc23

First Edition

Published in 2021 by
Gareth Stevens Publishing
111 East 14th Street, Suite 349
New York, NY 10003

Designer: Sarah Liddell
Editor: Therese Shea

Photo credits: Cover, pp. 1, 17 mark reinstein/Shutterstock.com; background texture used throughout Lukasz Szwaj/Shutterstock.com; p. 5 Vlad G/Shutterstock.com; p. 7 (James Madison) American School/Art Images/Getty Images; p. 7 (Constitution) Earthsound/Wikimedia Commons; p. 9 warasit phothisuk/Shutterstock.com; p. 11 Aaron P. Bernstein/Stringer/Getty Images News/Getty Images; p. 13 Drew Angerer/Staff/Getty Images News/Getty Images; p. 15 photo courtesy of the Library of Congress; p. 19 JIM WATSON/Contributor/AFP/Getty Images; p. 21 Cameron Davidson/Photographer's Choice/Getty Images Plus/Getty Images; p. 23 adamkaz/E+/Getty Images; p. 25 Ben Jeayes/Shutterstock.com; p. 27 Sean Locke Photography/Shutterstock.com.

Printed in the United States of America

Some of the images in this book illustrate individuals who are models. The depictions do not imply actual situations or events.

CPSIA compliance information: Batch #CS20GS: For further information contact Gareth Stevens, New York, New York at 1-800-542-2595.

CONTENTS

WORDS IN THE GLOSSARY APPEAR IN **BOLD** TYPE THE FIRST TIME THEY ARE USED IN THE TEXT.

FIGHTING FOR FREEDOMS

Is it too much to expect rights and fair treatment from your government? The British colonists in America didn't think so in the 1700s. Years of asking for exactly that led to the American Revolution, a war for independence from Great Britain.

Winning that war in 1783 was the first step. What came next was just as important to the future of the new country. Figuring out how the nation would be organized, how it would make laws, and how it would carry them out had its own share of challenges and risks.

A new government was created, and it was called the "American experiment" for a reason! One feature of the new system was a must. The American people would finally get the representation in government they'd wanted—the U.S. Congress.

A CLOSER LOOK

THE ARTICLES OF **CONFEDERATION** (1781–1789) WAS THE FIRST U.S. CONSTITUTION, THE NAME FOR THE BASIC LAWS OF A NATION. THE ARTICLES HELD THE COUNTRY TOGETHER, BUT WAS WEAK OVERALL. SOMETIMES STATES IGNORED IT!

THE FIRST CONGRESSES

The First Continental Congress was formed in 1774 from delegates of 12 of the 13 colonies. Its purpose was presenting grievances, or complaints, and trying to reach an agreement with the British king, George III. The American Revolution broke out before the meeting of the Second Continental Congress. This body met from 1775 until 1781. The congress that followed was the Confederation Congress, after the name of the nation's first constitution—the Articles of Confederation.

GEORGE WASHINGTON CHOSE THE DESIGN FOR THE CAPITOL IN 1793. CONGRESS MEETS IN THIS BUILDING THAT HAS MORE THAN 600 ROOMS AND OVER 1.5 MILLION SQUARE FEET (139,000 SQ M).

A NEW WAY OF DOING THINGS

In 1787, 55 delegates met in Philadelphia, Pennsylvania, for a "Grand Convention" to fix the Articles of Confederation. This became known as the Constitutional Convention.

James Madison created a plan to split the federal, or national, government into three separate but equal branches. Each kept the others from holding too much power through a system of checks and balances. The legislature (a body of elected members) would make the laws, the executive (a president and other officials) would enforce them, and the judiciary (the courts) would interpret them.

Debates over power, voting, citizenship, foreign policy, finances, and more took place over several months. The result was the U.S. Constitution. It was made up of seven main parts called articles. Article I focused on Congress, the legislative, or lawmaking, branch of the government.

BREAKDOWN OF THE U.S. CONSTITUTION'S ARTICLE I

SECTIONS 1–3: WHAT CONGRESS IS

SECTIONS 4–7: HOW CONGRESS WORKS

SECTIONS 8–10: POWERS AND LIMITATIONS OF CONGRESS

SEPARATE STATES

Before the U.S. Constitution, states made many of their own laws, used their own forms of money, and often treated other states like foreign countries. Deciding which powers the states should keep and which should belong to the federal, or national, government was hard. Convincing independence-minded Americans to support a strong federal government was another challenge. The Constitution was printed and shared in every state. Citizens debated, wrote about, and even sang about it.

JAMES MADISON, LATER THE FOURTH PRESIDENT, BECAME KNOWN AS THE FATHER OF THE CONSTITUTION.

A CLOSER LOOK

THE CONSTITUTION BEGINS, **"WE THE PEOPLE . . ."** THIS TELLS AMERICANS THE COUNTRY BELONGS TO THEM. A CAPITAL LETTER STARTS "PEOPLE" AND OTHER NOUNS IN THE CONSTITUTION BECAUSE IT WAS A WRITING STYLE AT THE TIME.

SECTIONS 1–3: ESTABLISHING THE CONGRESS

Sections 1 through 3 of Article I explain Congress and who makes up its membership. Conflict about these ideas almost tore the Constitutional Convention apart. Small states wanted "one state, one vote" in Congress so their concerns weren't overshadowed. But states with more people wanted representation based on population.

Finally, the Great Compromise was reached. Section 1 states: **"ALL LEGISLATIVE POWERS . . . SHALL BE VESTED IN A CONGRESS OF THE UNITED STATES, WHICH SHALL CONSIST OF A SENATE AND HOUSE OF REPRESENTATIVES."** The Senate holds two members per state, while the House's membership is based on a state's population. Section 2 ordered an **"ENUMERATION,"** or **census**, to be held within three years. A census is held **"WITHIN EVERY SUBSEQUENT [FOLLOWING] TERM OF TEN YEARS"** to update the number of representatives.

A CLOSER LOOK

A 1929 ACT CAPPED THE NUMBER OF MEMBERS IN THE HOUSE OF REPRESENTATIVES AT 435. CENSUS RESULTS SHIFT THOSE 435 REPRESENTATIVES IF NEEDED, SO STATES MAY GAIN OR LOSE MEMBERS.

THE THREE-FIFTHS COMPROMISE

Hundreds of thousands of slaves lived in the United States at the time of the Constitutional Convention. They weren't considered citizens. Southern delegates wanted them included in state populations so they would have more representatives in Congress. Northern delegates were against this, some because they hated slavery and others because they feared the South's power. Eventually the "three-fifths compromise" was reached: Each enslaved individual counted as three-fifths of a person in that state's population.

YOU CAN VISIT THE ROOM AT INDEPENDENCE HALL IN PHILADELPHIA WHERE THE DELEGATES WHO WROTE THE CONSTITUTION, CALLED FRAMERS, SHAPED THE HIGHEST LAW IN THE UNITED STATES.

Not just anyone can join Congress. Section 2 states: "NO PERSON SHALL BE A REPRESENTATIVE WHO SHALL NOT HAVE ATTAINED TO [REACHED] THE AGE OF TWENTY-FIVE YEARS, AND BEEN SEVEN YEARS A CITIZEN OF THE UNITED STATES." The framers wanted House membership open to a wider range of the population. The rules aren't as strict as those for the Senate, included in Section 3: "NO PERSON SHALL BE A SENATOR WHO SHALL NOT HAVE ATTAINED TO THE AGE OF THIRTY YEARS, AND BEEN NINE YEARS A CITIZEN OF THE UNITED STATES."

The citizenship requirement was meant to discourage foreign countries from sending people to join Congress in order to influence the United States. The framers wanted immigrants, or those who came to settle there, to participate in government. However, they had to wait to do so.

THE POWER OF IMPEACHMENT

Sections 2 and 3 outline Congress's role in impeachment, or the act of charging someone with misconduct in office. "THE HOUSE OF REPRESENTATIVES . . . SHALL HAVE THE SOLE POWER OF IMPEACHMENT," **while** "THE SENATE SHALL HAVE THE SOLE POWER TO TRY ALL IMPEACHMENTS." **Any federal official can be impeached. The House examines evidence and recommends if the Senate should hold a trial. Three presidents have been impeached: Andrew Johnson in 1868, Bill Clinton in 1998, and Donald Trump in 2019.**

AT LEAST 13 PERCENT OF THOSE SWORN IN AT THE START OF THE 116TH CONGRESS IN JANUARY 2019 WERE IMMIGRANTS OR CHILDREN OF IMMIGRANTS. THERE WERE 52 IN THE HOUSE AND 16 IN THE SENATE.

A CLOSER LOOK

ARTICLE I SAYS THAT SENATORS ARE CHOSEN BY A STATE'S LEGISLATURE. IN 1913, THE SEVENTEENTH AMENDMENT CHANGED THAT. AN AMENDMENT IS A CHANGE OR ADDITION TO A CONSTITUTION. SENATORS ARE NOW ELECTED BY **POPULAR VOTE**.

According to Sections 2 and 3, every member of Congress must be "AN INHABITANT [RESIDENT] OF THAT STATE" where they were elected. Living in the same community as the citizens they represent means they're likely familiar with the needs of the area.

Section 2 talks about the voters: "THE ELECTORS IN EACH STATE SHALL HAVE THE QUALIFICATIONS REQUISITE [NECESSARY] FOR ELECTORS OF THE MOST NUMEROUS BRANCH OF THE STATE LEGISLATURE." This means that the people ("electors") who can vote for members of Congress must meet the standards set by their states for state legislature elections. In the 18th century, most states limited who could vote. Women, slaves, some free black Americans, Native Americans, and some white men who didn't own property were barred from participating in state—and therefore national—elections.

A CLOSER LOOK

IN 1870, THE FIFTEENTH AMENDMENT UPDATED SECTION 2, GIVING AFRICAN AMERICAN MEN THE RIGHT TO VOTE. WOMEN HAD TO WAIT ANOTHER 50 YEARS UNTIL THE NINETEENTH AMENDMENT DID THE SAME FOR THEM.

DOUBLE DUTY . . . SOMETIMES

Section 3 states, "THE VICE PRESIDENT OF THE UNITED STATES SHALL BE PRESIDENT OF THE SENATE." However, the vice president now focuses on executive branch duties and a "PRESIDENT PRO TEMPORE" ("president for a time") handles the day-to-day running of the Senate. The position is usually given to the longest-serving senator from the majority party, or the political party with the most members in the Senate. The vice president becomes the Senate president on special occasions and for tie-breaking votes, however.

ONCE BARRED FROM VOTING OR HOLDING OFFICE, WOMEN NOW HAVE MAJOR ROLES IN THE U.S. GOVERNMENT. NANCY PELOSI MADE HISTORY IN 2007 AS THE FIRST WOMAN ELECTED AS SPEAKER OF THE HOUSE, THE LEADER OF THE HOUSE OF REPRESENTATIVES.

SECTIONS 4 AND 5: ELECTIONS AND RULES

Section 4 of Article I focuses on elections. It declares that "THE TIMES, PLACES AND MANNER OF HOLDING ELECTIONS . . . SHALL BE PRESCRIBED [ARRANGED] IN EACH STATE BY THE LEGISLATURE THEREOF," but Congress can "MAKE OR ALTER SUCH REGULATIONS." This guarantees federal laws can override state ones. The framers were concerned states might refuse to recognize federal authority and not hold elections. This section gives Congress power to oversee some election processes too.

Section 5 states that in Congress: "EACH HOUSE MAY DETERMINE THE RULES OF ITS PROCEEDINGS, PUNISH ITS MEMBERS FOR DISORDERLY BEHAVIOR, AND . . . EXPEL A MEMBER." Congress decides how it will run itself. It chooses what rules its members must follow as well as what happens if rules are broken.

A FULL-TIME COMMITMENT

The framers set up the day-to-day operations of Congress in ways that made sense in the 18th century. Back then, travel was harder, communication was slower, and members had other jobs that kept them busy. "THE CONGRESS SHALL ASSEMBLE AT LEAST ONCE IN EVERY YEAR," **Section 4 directs. The first Monday in December was the chosen date. Congress now meets regularly, and members stay much of the year in Washington, DC. It's a full-time job!**

STATES HAVEN'T ALWAYS FOLLOWED THE CONSTITUTION'S RULES DURING ELECTIONS. SOME POLICIES MADE IT HARDER FOR CERTAIN PEOPLE, OFTEN **MINORITIES**, TO CAST THEIR VOTES. THE VOTING RIGHTS ACT WAS PASSED IN 1965 TO FIGHT THIS.

A CLOSER LOOK

TWENTY SENATORS AND FIVE REPRESENTATIVES HAVE BEEN EXPELLED FROM CONGRESS. PLENTY MORE HAVE BEEN DISCIPLINED FOR BAD BEHAVIOR TOO.

SECTION 6: PAYMENT AND PROTECTION

According to Section 6, members of Congress **"SHALL RECEIVE A COMPENSATION [MONEY] FOR THEIR SERVICES . . . PAID OUT OF THE TREASURY OF THE UNITED STATES."** That salary reinforces that their duty is to the federal government, which pays them, not to their state. It also avoids the problem of states refusing to pay their elected officials if they don't like how they're governing.

Congress can't do its job if members feel threatened, so **"THEY SHALL IN ALL CASES, EXCEPT TREASON, FELONY [SERIOUS CRIME] AND BREACH [DISTURBING] OF THE PEACE, BE PRIVILEGED FROM ARREST DURING THEIR ATTENDANCE AT THE SESSION OF THEIR RESPECTIVE HOUSES."** They also can't be arrested **"FOR ANY SPEECH OR DEBATE IN EITHER HOUSE."** The ability to speak and debate freely is critical for Congress to function properly.

A CLOSER LOOK

IN 1789, THE FRAMERS APPROVED PAYMENT OF ABOUT $6 FOR EACH DAY A MEMBER ATTENDED A SESSION OF CONGRESS. IN 2018, MOST MEMBERS OF CONGRESS RECEIVED A YEARLY SALARY OF $174,000.

ONE JOB AT A TIME

Another clause, or part, of Section 6 prevents members from serving in Congress while holding almost any other federal office: "NO SENATOR OR REPRESENTATIVE SHALL, DURING THE TIME FOR WHICH HE WAS ELECTED, BE APPOINTED TO ANY CIVIL OFFICE." This keeps presidents from having too much influence over someone serving in the executive and legislative branch. It also keeps the congressperson from making another job more appealing, like by approving a pay raise, and grabbing it for themselves.

THE HOUSE AND SENATE EACH HAVE THEIR OWN CHAMBER IN WHICH THEY CONDUCT THEIR BUSINESS, INCLUDING THEIR DEBATES.

SECTION 7: MAKING LAWS

Legislating is the primary purpose of Congress, but it has to work together with the president to pass laws. Section 7 explains the lawmaking process: **"EVERY BILL WHICH SHALL HAVE PASSED THE HOUSE OF REPRESENTATIVES AND THE SENATE, SHALL, BEFORE IT BECOME A LAW, BE PRESENTED TO THE PRESIDENT OF THE UNITED STATES; IF HE APPROVE HE SHALL SIGN IT, BUT IF NOT HE SHALL RETURN IT."**

A bill must pass through several steps in both chambers before it gets to the president. If the president signs the bill, it becomes a law. If the president vetoes, or rejects, the bill, it goes back to Congress for more debates. If it passes by two-thirds of the votes in each chamber in this second round of voting, it becomes a law.

GROUP WORK

Committees like the ones today weren't part of the framers' original vision, but they've become an important part of the lawmaking process. Thousands of bills are proposed every session of Congress, so committees divide up the workload. Each specializes in a subject, such as the national budget or the military. They decide if the bill is worth considering, gather information, hold hearings, make changes to the bill, and send it to the full chamber for debate.

HOW A BILL BECOMES A LAW

A BILL IS INTRODUCED IN THE HOUSE OR SENATE.

IT GOES TO ONE OR MORE COMMITTEES FOR REVIEW AND CHANGES.

IF THE COMMITTEE PASSES THE BILL, THE WHOLE CHAMBER VOTES ON IT.

IF IT PASSES IN THE CHAMBER, THE BILL GOES TO THE OTHER CHAMBER OF CONGRESS.

THE BILL AGAIN GOES TO A COMMITTEE FOR REVIEW AND CHANGES.

IF IT PASSES IN THE COMMITTEE, THE WHOLE CHAMBER VOTES ON THE BILL.

ALL CHANGES MUST BE APPROVED BY BOTH CHAMBERS OF CONGRESS.

AFTER THE BILL PASSES IN BOTH CHAMBERS, IT GOES TO THE PRESIDENT.

THE PRESIDENT SIGNS THE BILL INTO LAW OR VETOES IT.

IF THE BILL IS VETOED AND CONGRESS IS IN SESSION, IT CAN STILL BECOME A LAW IF TWO-THIRDS OF BOTH CHAMBERS VOTE FOR IT.

IF THE PRESIDENT REFUSES TO SIGN OR VETO A BILL, IT BECOMES A LAW AFTER 10 DAYS IF CONGRESS IS IN SESSION. IF CONGRESS ISN'T IN SESSION AFTER 10 DAYS, THE BILL DIES. THIS IS CALLED A POCKET VETO.

A CLOSER LOOK

AS OF JANUARY 2020, THERE HAVE BEEN 2,580 PRESIDENTIAL VETOES. SEVERAL PRESIDENTS DIDN'T USE THIS POWER AT ALL. THE LONGEST-SERVING PRESIDENT, FRANKLIN D. ROOSEVELT, HAD THE MOST WITH 635 VETOES. CONGRESS HAS MADE 111 VETOED BILLS INTO LAWS.

SECTION 8: MORE POWERS

Specific powers are given to the legislative branch of the U.S. government for the sake of convenience as well as for unity among the states and across the country. A wide range of powers are covered in Article I's Section 8, including:

- money: collecting taxes, borrowing funds, creating money, regulating trade, punishing **counterfeiting**
- postal system: establishing offices and roads for postal workers' use
- science and art: protecting the work of scientists and artists by making laws about **copyrights** and patents
- military: declaring war, creating an army and a navy

Congress is also in charge of governing the national capital (eventually Washington, DC), or **"THE SEAT OF THE GOVERNMENT OF THE UNITED STATES."** But the District of Columbia Home Rule Act of 1973 gives local elected officials some control over DC's affairs.

THE NECESSARY AND PROPER CLAUSE

But what good are powers if there's no way to enforce them? That's why the last part of Section 8 is so important. It gives Congress authority to do what's required to exercise its powers: "TO MAKE ALL LAWS WHICH SHALL BE NECESSARY AND PROPER FOR CARRYING INTO EXECUTION THE FOREGOING POWERS, AND ALL OTHER POWERS VESTED BY THIS CONSTITUTION IN THE GOVERNMENT OF THE UNITED STATES." Congress has used this clause to create many laws.

PIERRE L'ENFANT, A FRENCHMAN WHO FOUGHT FOR THE COLONIES DURING THE REVOLUTION, DESIGNED THE LAYOUT FOR WASHINGTON, DC, IN 1791.

A CLOSER LOOK

THE FIRST PATENT WENT TO SAMUEL HOPKINS IN 1790 FOR A PROCESS FOR MAKING POTASH (AN INGREDIENT IN FERTILIZER). MORE THAN 10 MILLION MORE PATENTS HAVE BEEN ISSUED SINCE!

SECTION 9: WHAT CONGRESS CAN'T DO

The framers put limits on Congress too. These restrictions are discussed in Section 9. One part says, **"THE PRIVILEGE OF THE WRIT OF HABEAS CORPUS SHALL NOT BE SUSPENDED."** The writ of habeas corpus is the requirement that an arrested person be brought before a judge or court before being put in prison. The Constitution forbids Congress from ending this right with a few extreme exceptions, such as an invasion.

There are restrictions on taxes too, such as: **"NO TAX OR DUTY SHALL BE LAID ON ARTICLES EXPORTED FROM ANY STATE."** So, goods moving from state to state for sale can't be taxed. Also **"A REGULAR STATEMENT AND ACCOUNT OF THE RECEIPTS AND EXPENDITURES OF ALL PUBLIC MONEY SHALL BE PUBLISHED FROM TIME TO TIME"** means Congress must show how money is spent.

A CLOSER LOOK

THE SIXTEENTH AMENDMENT SUPERSEDED, OR TOOK THE PLACE OF, A PART OF SECTION 9 THAT FORBIDS CONGRESS FROM CREATING DIRECT TAXES WITHOUT A CENSUS FIRST. THE AMENDMENT ALLOWS CONGRESS TO TAX PEOPLE'S INCOMES.

PARTY TIME

There's nothing in the Constitution about political parties, but they've shaped our country since its beginnings. Federalists and Democratic-Republicans disagreed about limits to federal power. Now, Democrats and Republicans compete for control over what bills are voted on, who's in charge of committees, who leads the House and Senate, and more. The framers were worried about members caring about their states more than the country, but loyalty to party is now one of the strongest forces.

ANOTHER PART OF SECTION 9 FORBIDS THE U.S. GOVERNMENT FROM SUPPORTING "THE PORTS OF ONE STATE OVER THOSE OF ANOTHER." STATES FEARED THE FEDERAL GOVERNMENT MIGHT FAVOR CERTAIN AREAS OF THE COUNTRY, GIVING THEM GREATER ECONOMIC SUCCESS.

Section 9 includes the **appropriations** clause: "NO MONEY SHALL BE DRAWN FROM THE TREASURY, BUT IN CONSEQUENCE OF APPROPRIATIONS MADE BY LAW." While Congress decides how government money is spent, it must pass tax legislation to do it. This makes sure that Congress exercises responsibility over the nation's money. This is called the "power of the purse." It's also part of the government's system of checks and balances.

To prevent foreign powers from influencing government, Congress's approval is needed if a government official wants to accept "ANY PRESENT, **EMOLUMENT**, OFFICE, OR TITLE, OF ANY KIND WHATEVER, FROM ANY KING, PRINCE, OR FOREIGN STATE." And if any official is looking for a fancy title, like duke or duchess, they're out of luck: "NO TITLE OF NOBILITY SHALL BE GRANTED BY THE UNITED STATES."

SLAVERY AND POLITICS

To encourage slaveholding states to approve the Constitution, the slave trade continued until 1808 through Section 9: "THE MIGRATION OR IMPORTATION OF SUCH PERSONS AS ANY OF THE STATES NOW EXISTING THINK PROPER TO ADMIT, SHALL NOT BE PROHIBITED [BANNED] BY THE CONGRESS PRIOR TO THE YEAR ONE THOUSAND EIGHT HUNDRED AND EIGHT." **The children of slaves continued to make up the enslaved population. Slavery remained legal in some states until the Thirteenth Amendment ended it in 1865.**

CONGRESS MAY DECIDE HOW MONEY WILL BE USED, BUT THE SECRETARY OF THE TREASURY USUALLY DECIDES WHAT IT LOOKS LIKE AND WHO IS ON IT. ONE RULE IS THAT NO ONE CURRENTLY ALIVE CAN APPEAR ON IT.

A CLOSER LOOK

THE FRAMERS MIGHT NOT HAVE IMAGINED FORMER SLAVES SERVING IN CONGRESS, BUT SEVERAL DID AFTER THE END OF THE AMERICAN CIVIL WAR (1861–1865).

SECTION 10: COUNTRY OVER STATE

The final section of Article I limits the power of the states. It maintains that certain powers only belong to the federal government. States are forbidden to **"ENTER INTO ANY TREATY, ALLIANCE, OR CONFEDERATION," "COIN MONEY," "GRANT ANY TITLE OF NOBILITY,"** and several other actions that could weaken the authority of the national government.

To guarantee that states won't act independently, they need Congress's consent to **"ENTER INTO ANY AGREEMENT OR COMPACT WITH ANOTHER STATE, OR WITH A FOREIGN POWER, OR ENGAGE IN WAR."** They can't maintain their own military by **"KEEP[ING] TROOPS, OR SHIPS OF WAR IN TIME OF PEACE."** However, a state can act on its own if **"ACTUALLY INVADED."** In the days of slower communication, this exception made sense.

A CLOSER LOOK

A COMMITTEE OF DETAIL PIECED TOGETHER THE FIRST DRAFT OF THE CONSTITUTION BASED ON THE CONVENTION DEBATES. AFTER FEEDBACK FROM DELEGATES, THE COMMITTEE OF STYLE POLISHED THE LANGUAGE INTO ITS FINAL FORM.

OOPS!

Soon after it was created, the Constitution was reproduced, by hand and by printing machines. These copies contained errors like words left out, ink marks, misspellings, **punctuation** problems, and even factual errors. Some words that look misspelled to us were accepted ways of spelling at that time, such as "Pensylvania." Different copies of the Constitution floated around the country for decades. An official version of the U.S. Constitution was finally issued in 1847.

THE CONSTITUTION IS WRITTEN ON PARCHMENT, WHICH IS ANIMAL SKIN THAT HAS GONE THROUGH A PROCESS TO PREPARE IT FOR WRITING OR PRINTING. PARCHMENT WAS OFTEN USED FOR IMPORTANT WRITINGS BECAUSE IT'S STRONG AND LONG-LASTING.

THE VOICE OF THE PEOPLE

Since the Constitution was written over 230 years ago, some parts have worked well and others haven't. Some have been changed through amendments, and some may be amended in the future.

However, the overall vision of the framers has endured in Article I. Those who represent American citizens in Congress still earn those positions through regular and fair elections. If they don't serve well enough, they may not be reelected or even be removed from office. Congress continues to be a separate-but-equal branch of the federal government tasked with many vital jobs. The American colonists wanted representation in government so much that they went to war for it. Article I contains many of their hopes for their new nation. The American experiment was a success!

A CLOSER LOOK

IN HIS 1863 GETTYSBURG ADDRESS, PRESIDENT ABRAHAM LINCOLN MADE FAMOUS THE PHRASE "GOVERNMENT OF THE PEOPLE, BY THE PEOPLE, FOR THE PEOPLE." HE WAS REMINDING PEOPLE ABOUT THE PRINCIPLES OF THE UNITED STATES, WHICH ARE REFLECTED IN THE CONSTITUTION.

NOT AN EXACT REFLECTION

The original members of Congress were white and male. That's no longer the case. However, Congress still doesn't reflect the nation's makeup. For example, in 2019, 39 percent of the U.S. population was nonwhite, yet nonwhites made up only 22 percent of Congress. While 51 percent of the population were women, only 24 percent of Congress members were women. Additionally, 14 percent of the population was born in a foreign country, yet only 3 percent of Congress was foreign-born.

HISTORIC FIRSTS IN U.S. CONGRESS

1789 THE FIRST U.S. CONGRESS MET IN NEW YORK CITY.

1790 CONGRESS BEGAN TO MEET IN PHILADELPHIA.

1797 SENATOR WILLIAM BLOUNT OF TENNESSEE WAS THE FIRST FEDERAL OFFICIAL TO BE IMPEACHED.

1800 CONGRESS MOVED TO WASHINGTON, DC.

1845 DAVID LEVY YULEE BECAME THE FIRST JEWISH PERSON TO SERVE IN THE SENATE.

1868 PRESIDENT ANDREW JOHNSON WAS THE FIRST PRESIDENT TO BE IMPEACHED, BUT WASN'T REMOVED FROM OFFICE BY THE SENATE.

1870 HIRAM REVELS OF MISSISSIPPI BECAME THE FIRST BLACK SENATOR.

1877 ROMUALDO PACHECO OF CALIFORNIA BECAME THE FIRST HISPANIC AMERICAN REPRESENTATIVE.

1907 CHARLES CURTIS OF KANSAS BECAME THE FIRST NATIVE AMERICAN SENATOR.

1917 JEANNETTE RANKIN OF MONTANA BECAME THE FIRST FEMALE CONGRESSWOMAN.

1929 THE PERMANENT APPORTIONMENT ACT SET THE NUMBER OF REPRESENTATIVES AT 435.

1957 DALIP SINGH SAUND OF CALIFORNIA BECAME THE FIRST ASIAN AMERICAN CONGRESSMAN.

2007 NANCY PELOSI, A REPRESENTATIVE FROM CALIFORNIA, WAS THE FIRST WOMAN ELECTED SPEAKER OF THE HOUSE.

2018 ILHAN OMAR (MINNESOTA) AND RASHIDA TLAIB (MICHIGAN) BECAME THE FIRST MUSLIM WOMEN ELECTED TO CONGRESS.

GLOSSARY

alliance: a union between people, groups, or countries

appropriation: an amount of money used by a government for a certain purpose

census: the official process of counting the number of people and collecting information about them

confederation: a group of people or states that support each other and act together

copyright: the legal right to be the only one to reproduce, publish, and sell a book, recording, or something else for a time period

counterfeit: made to look like something in order to trick people. Also, to make a copy of something, such as money, in order to trick people.

debate: an argument or public discussion. Also, having to do with formal public discussion or argument.

emolument: earnings or profit from employment

expenditure: the amount of money spent on something

hearing: a meeting at which evidence and arguments are presented to a person or group who will decide on an action

minority: describing people who are not part of the main group of a society. In the United States, African Americans, Native Americans, Latinos, and the poor are minority groups.

popular vote: the votes of all people in a country, rather than the votes of a group such as the Electoral College

punctuation: the marks, such as periods (.) and commas (,), that are used to make the meaning of a piece of writing clear

FOR MORE INFORMATION

BOOKS

Demuth, Patricia Brennan. *What Is the Constitution?* New York, NY: Penguin Workshop, 2018.

Hillard, Stephane. *The U.S. Capitol: The History of U.S. Congress.* New York, NY: PowerKids Press, 2018.

Steinkraus, Kyla. *Constitution.* Vero Beach, FL: Rourke Educational Media, 2015.

WEBSITES

The Constitution of the United States
www.archives.gov/founding-docs/constitution
See the original document, read about how it was created, and learn more interesting facts.

The U.S. House of Representatives and Senate
house.gov
senate.gov
Search for the members of Congress who represent where you live.

Welcome to the U.S. Capitol
www.visitthecapitol.gov
Explore more about Congress and the building it works in.

INDEX